Other Books by Lisa Birnbach

The Official Preppy Handbook

Lisa Birnbach College Books

Going to Work

Loose Lips

Other Books by Ann Hodgman

My Baby-sitter Is a Vampire (series)

Stinky Stanley (series)

Beat This!

Beat That!

Other Books by Patricia Marx

How to Regain Your Virginity

You Can Never Go Wrong by Lying

Blockbuster

Now Everybody Really Hates Me

Now I Will Never Leave the Dinner Table

How to Survive Junior High

Meet My Staff

Other Books by David Owen

High School

None of the Above

The Man Who Invented Saturday Morning

The Walls Around Us

My Usual Game

1,003

Great Things About Getting Older

**Lisa Birnbach,
Ann Hodgman,
Patricia Marx,
David Owen**

MJF BOOKS
NEW YORK

Published by MJF Books
Fine Communications
Two Lincoln Square
60 West 66th Street
New York, NY 10023

1,003 Great Things About Getting Older
Library of Congress Catalog Card Number 99-74463
ISBN 1-56731-358-2

Copyright © 1997 by Lisa Birnbach, Ann Hodgman, Patricia Marx,
David Owen.

This edition published by arrangement with Andrews McMeel
Publishing.

Manufactured in the United States of America on acid-free paper

MJF Books and the MJF colophon are trademarks of Fine Creative
Media, Inc.

10 9 8 7 6 5 4 3 2 1

Great Things About Getting Older

It doesn't take so long
for summer to come again.

•

You've paid off
your student loans.

•

You don't have to worry
about which way hemlines
are going.

•

Gray hair has more body.

•

No more car pools.

•

The therapy is starting
to kick in.

•

If you were getting
younger instead of older,
everyone would hate you.

•

You can wear your
pants on top of
your stomach.

•

One martini
does the work of three.

•

You receive mail every day,
even if it's only
catalogs and bills.

•

It is still possible
to calculate your age
without the help of
carbon isotopes.

•

No more Twister
or Beernopoly.

•

Your arthritis
makes you less likely to lose
your wedding ring.

•

Mad-cow disease
has an incubation period
of up to fifty years.

•

Social Security operates
on a first-come,
first-served basis.

•

What's Great About Turning

1

Finally you're a number.

2

Double your age.

3

The end of
those terrible twos.

4

Toilet-trained for good.

5

Make gifts out of
Popsicle sticks at school.

6

Eligible to be picked as
the reincarnation of
the Panchen Lama,
second only to
the Dalai Lama as
Tibet's spiritual leader.

7

Grown-ups can no longer tell
secrets in front of you
by spelling the words.

8

Ready for cursive.

9

You've outgrown
the Power Rangers.

10

Double digits at last.

11

Taller than
your grandmother.

12

The age at which Lolita
met Humbert Humbert.

13

No longer a *pre*teen.

14

The age of Juliet.

15

Can be tried as an adult
in most states.

16

Operate a motor vehicle.

17

Unprotected sex with classmates
is still plenty safe.

18

Vote and drink,
drink and vote.

19

Dormitory livin'.

20

All moral issues are conveniently
black and white.

21

Throw away that fake ID.

22

The last year dating seems fun.

23

Weekends suddenly have meaning.

24

You still have your fastball.

25

A quarter century!

26

Not too late to move back in
with your parents.

27

Jimi Hendrix, Jim Morrison,
Janis Joplin, Kurt Cobain,
and John Keats were
all dead by now.

28
Retirement age in the NFL.

29
Last chance to buy life insurance
without a physical exam.

30
Who wants to be trusted?

31
Still pass for twenty-nine.

32
Last year you can enlist.

33

Age at which Jesus was crucified.

34

Still possible to find a plastic
surgeon who says you don't
need a total face-lift.

35

Age at which the Buddha
attained enlightenment.

36

In the fifteenth century,
most people your age were dead.

37

Time to think about the future
and buy a camcorder.

38

Too young to die of
natural causes.

39

Still thirty-something.

40

Time to give
golf a try.

41

Age at which Ted Williams
hit his 500th homer.

42

Senior management
considers you too young.

43

Halfway to retirement.

44

Sounds younger than
forty-three, oddly.

45

As close to forty as to fifty.

46

The golden age for adultery.

47

Twenty-fifth college reunion.

48

The peak of your earning power.

49

Age at which Julia Child
wrote her first major cookbook.

50

Finally old enough for
the Senior Tour.

51

Only thirty-three
in base sixteen.

52

One year for every card
in the deck.

53

Think of heartburn
as a diet opportunity.

54

With corrective surgery,
you can throw away
your bifocals.

55

Mortgage all paid off.

56

You can go to law school
and have a second
career in time
to write your own
complicated will.

57

Sell your old Mickey Mouse watch
for lots of money.

58

At least you're not a grandparent.

59

No penalty for withdrawing
from your IRA.

60

Thirty years since you
turned thirty.

61

Valued for your experience.

62

No tuition left to pay.

63

They call you Sonny
at AARP meetings.

64

Pick your own replacement.

65

Mandatory retirement party.

66

Sell Amway from
your own home.

67

Surprise everyone by
having a midlife crisis *now.*

68

At this age, Satchel Paige was still
in his forties.

69

Dental implants let you
eat corn on the cob again.

70

Why did sixty seem so old?

71

The big cruise,
and no one expects you
to carry your luggage.

72

George Bush skydives.

73

Age at which Ronald Reagan
was elected to
his second term.

74

Refilling the bird feeder
is a good morning's work.

75

Age at which Nelson Mandela
became president
of South Africa.

76

Age at which arthritis caused
Grandma Moses
to give up embroidery
for painting.

77

Age at which
Winston Churchill
became prime minister
for the second time.

78

From here to the end,
every year's a bonus.

79

You don't have to hit the ball—
just standing on the court
is enough.

80
Discounts at elderhostels.

81
This winter in Florida,
don't bother using
sunscreen.

82
The hit of your granddaughter's
wedding reception!

83
Just turn up your
hearing aid.

84

Just turn down your hearing aid.

85

Not too old to drive a great big car.

86

Use as much salt as you want.

87

Reruns seem like season premieres.

88

You can still identify half the people in your photo albums.

89

Raising your arms
counts as exercise.

90

The big time.

91

Why go outside
when you have
the Weather Channel?

92

Wild mushrooms are
now worth the risk.

93

Bingo as a spectator sport.

94

Someone else will
cut up your food.

95

A *Playboy* centerfold may
consider your offer of marriage.

96

You'll never be alone
in a bathroom again.

97

Your children are now retired.

98

If you were going to get
Alzheimer's,
you'd have it by now.

99

Might as well hang in there
for the big one.

100

All your enemies are dead.

You can correct others
without fear of
being corrected yourself.

•

No one questions you
if you take a sick day.

•

You get a seat
on the bus.

•

A little sex goes
a long way.

•

If it's raining,
no one expects you
to vote.

•

Come to think of it,
death will be kind
of a relief.

•

People pick up
the things you drop.

•

Boys don't snap
your bra.

•

Plenty of Kleenex
in your house
and on your person.

•

Your son can tie his own tie.

•

You knew who J.F.K. was
before the Oliver Stone
movie came out.

•

The most frighteningly
beautiful and popular girl
in your high school class
is now a blackjack dealer
in Atlantic City.

•

No one asks you how
you did on the SAT.

•

You may be eligible
to be a plaintiff in
age-discrimination suits.

•

You no longer feel obligated
to use chopsticks
in Chinese restaurants.

•

You can board airplanes first.

•

RuPaul is now
a grande dame.

•

Tipsy? Blame it on
the side effects of L-dopa.

•

More and more people
you hate are dead.

•

Being Young Isn't So Great

Having to fight off
embarrassing sexual come-ons

•

Acne

•

Needing permission

•

Firm, firm breasts:
how are you supposed to sleep?

•

Blood pressure ominously low

•

Dancing in public

•

Sexually transmitted diseases

•

Having parents

•

Losing a contact lens

•

Staying up until all hours

•

Troublesome erections

•

Always washing your sheets

•

One-year apartment leases

•

Prenuptial jitters

•

Having to figure out whether
no means yes

•

Finding outlets for all that energy

•

Passing the swimming test

•

Scary movies

•

Doc Martens

•

Applying to college

•

Long, lustrous hair
that gets stuck in everything

•

Body piercing

•

Twenty-twenty vision:
the better to see the horrors of life

•

Entry-level jobs

•

Childbirth

•

Black lipstick

•

Entertaining small children
on airplanes

•

Regrets the next morning

•

Roller coasters

•

Flimsy, expensive clothing

•

Hang-gliding accidents

•

Going off to war

•

Thigh-highs

•

Having a boss

•

Losing your keys
at the rock festival

•

Driving at night

•

Housebreaking puppies

•

Finding someone
to cosign that loan

•

Waiting for the StairMaster
to be free

•

The awkwardness
of having slept with
so many of your friends

•

Worrying how long
the keg will last

•

Sore muscles

•

Camping

•

Lending a hand
with anything heavy

•

Hangovers

•

Suddenly skinny-dipping

•

Not bringing
the right clothes

•

Deciding at three A.M. to drive
to Atlantic City

•

Broken toys

•

Piano lessons

•

Finding time to
spend your money

•

No more peewee
hockey games
to watch.

•

You get to read
the funnies first.

•

The Vermont Country Store
seems trendier every year.

•

You can throw away
the Christmas decorations
that your children made
in nursery school.

•

No more embarrassing
birds-and-bees discussions
with your kids.

•

You don't have to walk
in airports.

•

You feel free to criticize
the parenting skills of people
you don't know.

•

You know more than
enough Hebrew.

•

You are in less danger
of accidentally revealing
the truth about Santa Claus.

•

You can probably
beat up your father.

•

You might as well subscribe
to *Reader's Digest.*

•

So what if
the inheritance tax
is steep?

•

Foundation garments
become more comfortable
every year.

•

People get out of
your way when
you drive down the street.

•

Juries are less likely
to sentence you to death.

•

You remove mattress tags
without fear of
legal consequences.

•

You don't have to swim
when the water is colder
than ninety degrees.

•

No one will ask you
to substitute-teach.

•

Most Kids <u>Want</u> to Get Older

"You get a bigger allowance,
and when you get older, the boys are
older, so they can drive you to school."
—*Emily Stuart, age seven*

"Some things that I can't do now, but I
can do when I'm older, are going to college at Harvard or Duke, having my own
house, and owning a candy store so I
can feast on free candy whenever I like."
—*Jamie Leifer, age nine*

"Once I get to be
thirteen or fourteen,
I'll be able to walk
the dog myself."
—*Kate Radlauer, age eight*

"You can get your driver's license
and do lots more things,
like drink beer."
—*Teddy Stuart, age eleven*

"I'd like to be four some more.
That was my best, best year."
—*Louisa Winston, age nine*

"I want to get older
so I don't have to take my
Ritalin in the morning."
—*Lizzie Chase, age six*

"I am disgusted with the idea
of getting older, because the
afternoon chores get harder and it's
harder to find the pieces of dirt."
—*Sam Haft, age five*

"I would like to get older
so that I don't have a
wicked-early bedtime."
—*Mark Trumbull, age nine*

"You can spell words to other people."
—*Phoebe Carter, age five*

"I want to be older so I can have
a baby and eat as much
ice cream as I want."
—*Lucy Anderson, age six*

"When you get older, you get homework,
and that makes you learn."
—*Jessie Hornig, age five*

"When I'm old, I can pierce my ears."
—*Chloe Payne, age eight*

"A good thing
about getting older
is that you can like boys."
—*Julia Hornig, age nine*

"I want to be older so I can pay taxes."
—*Lisa Semple, age five*

"I'm not allowed to bite my baby
brother, pinch him, or color his face.
But when I'm bigger, I can."
—*Rachel Marx, age three*

"I want to be older so I can
make out checks and be
a millionaire."
—*John Semple, age seven*

"I want to be eighteen so I can drive
the littlest red convertible."
—*Max VanDam, age nine*

"Why am I not a grown-up?
I've been here for so many years."
—*Laura Owen, age four*

"When I grow up, I will go to a PG."
—*Avalon Nicholas Wolf, age four*

"At least I won't have to clear the table."
—*Hunter Stewart, age twelve*

What the hell?—
Send that swing set
to the dump.

•

Isaac Bashevis Singer
did not become famous
until he was in his fifties.

•

Your grandchildren will be
impressed that you lived in
the twentieth century.

•

You have nothing more to fear
from quicksand, avalanches,
or poison ivy.

•

You may qualify for
discounted "bereavement" rates
on air travel.

•

No more dead goldfish
to flush.

•

Now that you're retired,
you'll never be fired.

•

Your children can
brush their own teeth,
take out their own splinters,
and wipe their own bottoms.

•

You don't have to join in
friendly volleyball games.

•

You save on shampoo.

•

It's okay to cross
intersections slowly.

•

No one complains
if you eat the
last Popsicle
in the freezer.

•

You can hand out money
instead of candy at Halloween.

•

Sagging jowls
have made your cheekbones
more prominent.

•

Your ophthalmologist
may suggest marijuana
for your glaucoma.

•

Going to bed
is simpler now
that you can fall asleep
in your chair.

•

Philip Johnson
did not become
an architect until
he was thirty-nine.

•

Great Things That Older People Have Said About Getting Older

"The privilege . . . of being insolent
and supercilious without punishment."
—*William Pitt*

"The secret of staying young
is to live honestly, eat slowly,
and lie about your age."
—*Lucille Ball*

"Old age is always
fifteen years older than I am."
—*Bernard Baruch*

"A woman has the age she deserves."
—*Coco Chanel*

"The joy of being older
is that in one's life one can,
towards the end of the run,
overact appallingly."
—*Quentin Crisp*

"The great thing about being thirty
is that there are a great deal
more available women.
The young ones look younger and
the old ones don't look nearly as old."
—*Glenn Frey*

"The lovely thing about being forty
is that you can appreciate
twenty-five-year-old men more."
—*Colleen McCullough*

"The advantage
of being eighty years old
is that one has had
many people to love."
—*Jean Renoir*

"If you survive long enough,
you're revered
—rather like an old building."
—*Katharine Hepburn*

"Growing old is something you do
if you're lucky."
—*Groucho Marx*

"I love everything that's old:
old friends, old times,
old manners, old books, old wines."
—*Oliver Goldsmith*

"It has been said that
there is no fool
like an old fool,
except a young fool.
But the young fool
has first to grow up
to be an old fool
to realize what a damn fool
he was when he was a young fool."
—*Harold Macmillan*

"The older you get,
the faster you ran as a kid."
—*Steve Owen*

"Old age has a great
sense of calm and freedom;
when the passions relax
their hold, then . . .
we are freed from the grasp
not of one mad master only,
but of many."
—*Plato*

"When grace is joined with wrinkles,
it is adorable."
—*Victor Hugo*

"Senility is a convenient peg
on which to hang nonconformity."
—*Frances, a nursing home resident*

"Ripeness is all."
—*Shakespeare*

"I have made it a rule to go to bed when there wasn't anybody left to sit up with; and I have made it a rule to get up when I had to. . . . In the matter of diet . . . I have been persistent in sticking to the things which didn't agree with me until one or the other of us got the best of it. For thirty years I have taken coffee and bread at eight in the morning and no bite nor sup until seven-thirty in the evening. . . . I have made it a rule never to smoke more than one cigar at a time. . . . I smoke in bed until I have to go to sleep; I wake up in the night, sometimes once, sometimes twice, sometimes three times, and I never waste any of these opportunities to smoke. . . . As for drinking, I have no rule about that. When the others drink, I like to help; otherwise I remain dry, by habit and preference. . . .

Since I was seven years old I have seldom taken a dose of medicine, and have still sel-domer needed one. . . . I have never taken any exercise, except sleeping and resting, and I never intend to take any. Exercise is loathsome. And it cannot be any benefit when you are tired; and I was always tired."
—*Mark Twain*

"Age is biological,
but psychologically
when I am playing,
I feel like a young man.
My muscles have acquired
a wisdom of their own,
and I think they are working
better than ever."
—*Claudio Arrau*

"If artists realize their work is getting a
little too tight, they should try a new
touch in what they put on the canvas
and paint with a longer brush."
—*B. F. Skinner*

"That today is yesterday
and tomorrow is today you can't stop.
The body is your instrument in dance,
but your art is outside that creation,
the body. I don't leap or jump anymore.
I look at young dancers
and I am envious. More aware
of what glories the body contains.
But sensitivity is not made dull by age."
—*Martha Graham*

"The spiritual eyesight improves
as the physical eyesight declines."
—*Plato*

Need a day off? No one can
prove you don't have sciatica.

•

On a sinking boat, you'll be
saved with the women
and children.

•

A flight attendant
will help you put your bag
in the overhead compartment.

•

No more chaperoning.

•

You remember the last time
your company tried that idea,
and why it didn't work.

•

You can tell your friends
the same joke over
and over and over.

•

No reason not to stop
for green lights, too.

•

Nat "King" Cole revivals.

•

That wooden tennis racket
of yours may be
of interest to
the Smithsonian.

•

You don't have to
renew your subscription
to *Rolling Stone.*

•

You'll never again
have to drive a car
that's small enough
to parallel-park.

•

Diet no more! You're ready
for liposuction.

•

Fifty-year-olds
look more attractive to you.

•

You will never have to
watch your kids in
another talent show.

•

You get the taxi even
if you didn't see it first.

•

There's more of you to love,
especially the middle
part of you.

•

Charles Schulz
seems funny again.

•

People will help you
cross the street.

•

New Products for Older Customers

Raincoat Reminder

Distinguish your Burberry trench
coat from the hundreds of others
on the rack. Two versions:
electronic audio signal
and distinctive epaulet.
"A godsend."

— JOSEPH BOVELLO, *coatroom attendant,*
St. Mary's Main Street Cathedral

Caffeine-Alyzer

The answer to deceitful waiters
and waitresses. If the paper strip
turns green, there's too much
caffeine. Plain, or treated
with Sweet 'n Low.

Slow-Release Fiber Patch

Promotes regularity transdermally.
More effective than Metamucil,
and worth the extra cost.
Will not stain clothing.

The Original Neckcercycle

Turns gum-chewing into
an aerobic activity. Easy-to-clean
gears safely tone your jaw and
neck. Instructional video.

Kleenex Sleeve Pack

Slimline dispenser straps to your
wrist with gentle Velcro bands.
Fits inside most sweater sleeves.
Now you can always have a
Kleenex in your cuff.

No more
police lineups.

•

Dinner theater
seems like a
good entertainment
value.

•

You can judge clothing
mainly on the basis of its
elastic content.

•

Colonel Sanders was in his
sixties when he invented
Kentucky Fried Chicken.

•

You'll never have to be
a troop leader again.

•

You can borrow
your children's
razors and deodorant.

•

The trunk on a Cadillac
closes all by itself.

•

Evenings
at the country club.

•

Adult diapers
are actually
kind of convenient.

•

Air bags were designed
with you in mind.

•

It's easier to find
a radio station
you enjoy listening to.

•

It's been a long time
since anybody
called you a brat.

•

No more student council
elections.

•

Plenty of good mysteries
are available in
large-print editions.

•

You no longer have to travel
with your parents or
your children.

•

You can remember
when grown-ups were scared
of Mick Jagger.

•

Dessert seems
less important.

•

Maybe You Shoul

Here's how old you would be if you lived on:

Earth	**10**	**30**
Mercury	41	124
Venus	16	49
Mars	5	16
Jupiter	7 months	2.5
Saturn	5 months	1.2
Uranus	1 month	3 month
Neptune	Not even home from the hospital yet	2 month
Pluto	Zip	Negligibl

Move to Pluto

50	70	100
207	290	415
81	114	162
27	37	53
4	6	8.5
2	2.8	4
8 months	10 months	1
3 months	5 months	8 months
2 months	2.8 months	5 months

Kidnappers are not
very interested in you.

•

When you have a flat tire,
people aren't afraid
to stop to help you.

•

Stage fright
is no longer an issue.

•

You can make it through
an entire day without taking off
your slipper socks.

•

No more diving boards.

•

You have a steadily improving
chance of shooting
your age in golf,
at least for nine holes.

•

Golden Girls.

•

You know how
to write a lovely
condolence note.

•

Jonathan Swift
wrote *Gulliver's Travels*
when he was fifty-nine.

•

No more pop quizzes
or spelling tests.

•

You know the best kind
of silver polish.

•

You can stop being
a good sport.

•

Efferdent is good
for cleaning jewelry, too.

•

Having grandchildren
makes up for
not having grandparents.

•

Modern Maturity is a
pretty interesting magazine.

•

What does Jenny McCarthy
have that
Brigitte Bardot doesn't?

•

You can meet your kids
for drinks.

•

You can turn out the front light,
lock the door, and go to bed
when carolers come to call.

•

Now There Are So Many Ways to Describe Your Age

*If you are a woman of
a certain age, you are*

statuesque, handsome,
settled, a grande dame, stately,
spry, active, majestic,
well preserved, vigorous.

If you are a man of years, you are

solid, judicious, eminent,
strong, robust, veteran,
presidential, experienced,
measured, well traveled.

Just because you've gotten this far,
you are assumed to be

distinguished, venerable, wise,
authoritative, knowledgeable,
hard to fool, sensible, discerning,
not impetuous, enlightened,
prudent, comfortable.

Foods you don't like taste more
like foods you do.

•

Your luggage matches.

•

You may now
be ready for bow ties.

•

Spill all you like!
You won't be punished.

•

No one has to explain
to you why Sean Connery
is a celebrity.

•

You're living proof
of a cornerstone of science:
the law of gravity.

•

You've found a car mechanic
you can trust.

•

Saying you forgot
is enough of an excuse.

•

Nobody calls
the Beach Boys
the Beach Men.

•

No more sleeping
in tents.

•

Edward Hopper
was in his sixties
when he first became famous.

•

Dennis Hopper
is in his sixties
and is still making movies.

•

Nowadays, almost everything
comes with a remote control.

•

Using bad words
now makes you seem
delightfully wicked.

•

If you don't like the movie,
you can go to sleep.

•

The music in elevators
seems to have improved.

•

Why *do* we tax capital gains?

•

It's harder and harder
to make those
sexual-harassment
charges stick.

•

You don't have to
get all worked up about
New Year's Eve.

•

The Gold Mine in Your Attic

Somewhere in Your Attic
You Still Have . . .

Comic book in which
Superman rescues
Evelyn Curry from
electric chair (1938)
Recent Appraisal: $130,000

Pineapple Pez dispenser
Recent Appraisal: $750–$900

Beatles cake-decorating kit
Recent Appraisal: $195

Beatles yellow submarine
coin bank (set of four)
Recent Appraisal: $1,400

Barbie (1969, in box)
Recent Appraisal: $550

Barbie No. 1 (with brunette hair,
original ponytail, blue eyeliner,
red lips, finger and toe paint,
straight legs, gold earrings, white
swimsuit, and white glasses)
Recent Appraisal: $2,200

Monkees ring (flasher type)
Recent Appraisal: $30

Addams Family
board game (1974)
Recent Appraisal: $30

Barbie Queen of the Prom
board game (1960)
Recent Appraisal: $40

Dr. Seuss's Sleep Book
(first edition, 1962)
Recent Appraisal: $170

Hummel Cinderella
figurine (eyes open,
with LB mark, 1970)
Recent Appraisal: $720

Sea Hunt board game (complete)
Recent Appraisal: $45

Man from U.N.C.L.E. cards (1965)
Recent Appraisal: $20

Log Cabin syrup tin,
Dr. R. U. Well (cartoon style)
Recent Appraisal: $255

"Milk Cow Blues," Elvis Presley
(Absolutely mint condition 45)
Recent Appraisal: $1,000 plus

"I'm a Lonesome Baby,"
Ike Turner
(excellent condition)
Recent Appraisal: $7.50

Levine ankle boots, chartreuse
suede with red-and-white wedge
soles, never worn (1960s)
Recent Appraisal: $690

Men's platform shoes,
multicolored suede (1960s)
Recent Appraisal: $150

Dashiki (1970)
Recent Appraisal: $175

Howdy Doody ventriloquist doll
(1950s)
Recent Appraisal: $135

Tonka Truck, Allied Van Lines (1950s)
Recent Appraisal: $235

L'il Orphan Annie
pastry set (1930s)
Recent Appraisal: $140

Monopoly board game,
first edition, in original box
Recent Appraisal: $1,000

Gone With the Wind, with "printed
May 1936" on copyright page
Recent Appraisal: $200

Catcher in the Rye (first edition, 1951)
Recent Appraisal: $500

Fun with Dick and Jane (1946)
Recent Appraisal: $300

Mean old ladies yell
with you, not at you.

•

No more
dancing school.

•

You *can* buy friends.

•

Frank Sinatra records.

•

There's less and less chance
that you'll be dragged
from your house
and thrown into a
swimsuit competition.

•

You can weep openly
while watching
It's a Wonderful Life.

•

Decaffeinated cappuccino.

•

Dinner out costs less
if you eat
between four and six.

•

You're too old to be
the fourth-grade outcast.

•

If John Travolta
can make a comeback,
so can you.

•

Why wait for dark
to go to bed?

•

You will probably
be among the first hostages
to be released.

•

Closed-captioning
makes the evening news
seem like an exotic
foreign movie.

•

You can win the respect of
young people merely
by picking up the check.

•

You can sit back and
watch Sharon Stone
get wrinkly and gray.

•

Emily Post was in her late fifties
when she wrote her first
etiquette book.

•

Life Is (Now) Too Short for the Following, Thank Goodness

Planting trees

•

Reading anything in the original

•

Washing the good china by hand

•

Doing push-ups

•

Raking leaves

•

Buying the extended warranty

•

Restoring a wonderful old house

•

Changing planes in Chicago

•

Saving for a rainy day

•

Canning the extra blueberries

•

Learning how to back up
computer files

•

Hemming it yourself

•

Running for a bus

•

Learning a new language

•

Keeping down those
credit-card balances

•

Quitting smoking

•

Making new friends

•

Making sure your salt supplies
iodine, a necessary nutrient

•

Buying cheap paper towels

•

Teaching Sunday school

•

Reading Proust

•

Eating leftovers

•

Caring about
the Red Sox

•

Clarifying butter

•

Wrapping it yourself

•

Shoveling—or for that matter,
walking in—snow

•

Protecting your eyes during
solar eclipses

•

Wondering if you should have
gone to medical school instead

•

Saving old wrapping paper

•

Doing your own nails

•

Sending anything parcel post

•

Rotating your tires

•

Ironing

•

Folding

•

Voting

•

Eating at restaurants
that don't take reservations

•

Manual car windows

•

Staying up to greet the new year

•

Cloth napkins

•

Class participation

•

Buying unripe fruit

•

Keeping up with news of Asia

•

Owning too few pairs of scissors

•

Eating on the beach

•

Checking the nutritional
information

•

Buying new tires

•

Working to change the system
from within

•

Cleaning up your basement

•

Having exact change

•

Learning the names
of constellations other than
the Big Dipper

•

Throwing dinner parties

•

Margarine

•

Stewing about the mess in
Washington

•

Vacuuming under the bed.

•

Finding a better way to organize
your kitchen cupboards

•

Learning the name of your
new UPS man

•

Sending Christmas cards

•

Going to a movie
without reading the reviews first

•

Paper-training

•

Cutting down
your own Christmas tree

•

Saving the bones to make soup

•

Camping overnight
in the ticket-office parking lot

•

Driving a domestic car

•

Comparison shopping

•

RSVPing

•

Watching the Oscars

•

Using recipes
with more than four ingredients

•

Setting places with
more than one fork.

•

Improving your posture

•

Traveling to countries
where no one speaks English

•

Changing the message
on your answering machine

•

Moving

•

Living up to your potential

•

Sitting in the balcony

•

Turning the other cheek

•

Waiting for
double-value-coupon day

•

Weeding

•

Sharpening your negotiating skills

•

Finishing what you start

•

Using public transportation

•

Doing anything stand-by

•

Going back to get your degree

•

Traveling by bus

•

Putting children first

•

Holding the elevator

•

Waiting by the phone

•

Sharing desserts

•

Keeping a maintenance log

•

Driving a used car

•

Standing on ceremony

•

Standing

•

Painting it yourself

•

Thinking of names for pets

•

Having sex anywhere but bed

•

Potluck suppers

•

Memorizing state capitals

•

Checking your arithmetic

•

Saving the box it came in

•

Changing the battery in
a digital watch

•

Checking the unit price

•

Developing a firm handshake

•

Standing ovations

•

Finding the perfect wedding gift

•

Buying flood insurance

•

Sticking around for
coffee afterwards

•

Fighting the good fight

•

Sending anything back
to the factory for repairs

•

Learning a new instrument

•

Learning someone's name

•

Memorizing your children's
phone numbers

•

Getting the most
of what the city has to offer

•

Parallel parking

•

Stripping anything
down to the bare wood

•

Arguing about the overdue fee
on library books

•

Lifting heavy things

•

Dancing

•

Hurrying

•

Apologizing

•

A roll of Life Savers
in every purse.

•

You can't be drafted.
You can't even enlist.

•

You can sit down
at cocktail parties.

•

No one thinks you're lazy
if you pay someone else
to carry your
groceries to your car.

•

It's harder
to make you blush.

•

The collected works
of Cary Grant.

•

You get credit
just for showing up.

•

You finally know
what a bed jacket is.

•

Why not an elevator
in your house?

•

Infomercials
seem like real TV.

•

You are expected
to undertip.

•

Harry Truman
was first elected to
the Senate at the age
of fifty.

•

No one cares if you eat
Jell-O and melba toast
for dinner.

•

Joni Mitchell
compilations.

•

Your thighs are nobody's
business but your own.

•

There are lots of interesting
nature programs
on public television.

•

You can keep a dish of candy
on the coffee table.

•

Your investment in
health insurance
is beginning to pay off.

•

Great Things
to Say on
Your Deathbed

"I should have never switched
from Scotch to martinis."
—*Last words of Humphrey Bogart,*
1957

"Am I dying, or is this my birthday?"
—*Nancy Astor, 1964,*
on seeing her children gathered
around her bed during
her final illness

"Doctor, do you think
it could have been the sausage?"
—*Paul Claudel, 1953*

"That was the best
ice-cream soda I ever tasted."
—*Lou Costello, 1959*

"Good night, my darlings,
I'll see you tomorrow."
—*Noël Coward, 1976*

"It don't matter.
I figure I licked the Rock anyway."
—*Bernard Coy, 1946,*
after being shot while trying
to escape from Alcatraz

"That was a great
game of golf, fellers."
—*Bing Crosby, 1977*

"My fun days are over."
—*James Dean, 1955*

"I'm going for
the big time—heaven."
—*Andrea "Whips" Feldman, an
Andy Warhol superstar, before jumping
to her death from a window*

"I've had a hell of a lot of fun
and I've enjoyed every minute of it."
—*Errol Flynn, 1959*

"Let's do it!"
—*Gary Gilmore, 1977,*
to his firing squad

"Only suckers
get hit with right hands."
—*Charley Goldman,*
American boxing trainer, 1970

"I want to go out
in a puff of smoke
and take a few
policemen with me!"
—*Paul Howe,*
British teenage desperado, 1979

"I am fed up with living artificially.
I don't want to live like Tito."
—*The Shah of Iran, 1980*

"Let us go over the river
and sit in the shade
of the trees."
—*"Stonewall" Jackson, 1863*

"That's it. I'm going.
I'm going."
—*Al Jolson, 1950*

"Mind your own business."
—*Percy Wyndham Lewis, 1957*

"Cool it, brothers."
—*Malcolm X, 1966*

"Dying is a very dull, dreary affair.
My advice to you is
to have nothing whatsoever
to do with it."
—*W. Somerset Maugham, 1965*

"God, I'm bored."
—*St. John Philby, 1960*

"Drink to me."
—*Pablo Picasso, 1973*

"I hope I haven't bored you."
—*Elvis Presley, 1977,*
concluding his final
press conference

"Why yes, a bulletproof vest."
—*James Rodgers, 1960,*
upon being asked
if he had a last request
before meeting
his firing squad

"I have a terrific headache."
—*Franklin D. Roosevelt, 1945*

"All right, Mr. DeMille,
I'm ready for my close-up."
—*Gloria Swanson
as Norma Desmond,
1950, in the movie*
Sunset Boulevard

"God bless . . .
God damn . . ."
—*James Thurber, 1961*

"Go away. I'm all right."
—*H. G. Wells, 1946*

"So, this is death! Well!"
—*Ludwig van Beethoven, 1827*

"Either that wallpaper goes
or I do."
—*Oscar Wilde, 1900*

"Curtain! Fast music! Lights!
Ready for the last finale!
Great!
The show looks good.
The show looks good."
—*Florenz Ziegfeld, 1932*

"Now comes
the mystery."
—*Henry Ward Beecher, 1887*

Ramps.

•

You'll never need Cybercash.

•

You can afford wine
with dinner.

•

Your old car
now seems funky.

•

No more high heels.

•

The crummy shows you
watched as a kid
are now called the
Golden Age of Television.

•

If you've never smoked,
you can start now and
it won't have time to hurt you.

•

Bingo.

•

People no longer view you
as a hypochondriac.

•

Armani reading glasses.

•

Your clothes are
back in style.

•

Without your having to ask,
your husband stops drag racing.

•

Lying about your age is easier
now that you sometimes
forget what it is.

•

Programming your VCR for you
makes your grandchildren
feel good about themselves.

•

Handicapped parking spaces.

•

Paul Newman.

•

Laser plastic surgery
is no longer just a dream.

•

You can use your kids' rooms
for storage.

•

It's easier to
pick your teeth now—
just take them
out of your mouth
and hold them
up to the light.

•

You don't have
to sing along
if you don't want to.

•

Why You Owe It to Yourself to Die Poor

Many older Americans behave as though the purpose of having money is not to buy the boat they've always dreamed of but to ensure that their grandchildren will be able to fly business-class to their funeral. These older Americans have savings and investments worth hundreds of thousands of dollars, yet they drive an old Caprice that they bought secondhand from Hertz. They attend seminars on estate building—an oxymoron if ever there was one. They shop at Costco, reuse twist ties, and invest for long-term growth.

This behavior makes no sense. Why sacrifice now so that you can be wealthy when you're dead? Living isn't like eating in polite company; you don't have to leave something on your plate for Miss Manners. In fact, as closing time draws near, you should throw your spoon to the floor and slurp the last of the whipped cream from the bottom of your bowl.

No life can be said to have been lived to the fullest unless its final accounting takes place in bankruptcy court. Here's what you should do:

- *Cash in your life insurance.* You insured your life when you were young because you were worried that your kids might not get to college if anything happened to you. Well, nothing happened to you, and your children all have diplomas. More to the point, they've mentioned nothing about paying you back. Dump your policy and invest those premiums in your wine cellar.

- *Sell your house and rent a nice apartment.* Owning your home made sense when you were young. inflation turned your mortgage payments into chump change, and rising real estate values helped to make you rich. But now you're older. Remember: Owning is forever, but renting ends when you do.

- *Borrow, borrow, borrow.* If you don't want to sell your house, turn it from an asset into a liability. Take out the biggest mortgage you can, set aside just enough to cover the monthly payments between now and your estimated date of death (see Life Expectancy Table below), and spend, spend, spend. And don't forget those credit cards. Load them to the max and let the banks come after your children when you're gone.

- *Sell the family jewels.* If you hang on to your diamonds, your children will auction them off before your corpse is cold. Sell everything now and spend the proceeds on stuff that you can eat, drink, drive, or use up. Even Jackie O. wore cubic zirconia.

- *Touch the principal.* Never dipping into your personal endowment might be a good strategy if you were going to live forever. But you're not. Interest and dividends are for sissies. Start taking those capital gains.
- *Lose the funeral.* At $5,000 or so, a casket is the most expensive piece of furniture that most people ever buy. And what happens to it? It gets thrown in a hole and covered with dirt. Donate your body to Harvard and spend the savings *tomorrow* on a couple of weeks at Canyon Ranch.

The point of intelligent estate planning is to make sure that there will be no estate. This worksheet should help.

Die Poor Worksheet

1. Your current net worth (all your assets, including pensions and real estate, minus your liabilities, including mortgages and other debts)   _____

2. Round-trip New York–Paris airfare via the Concorde, for two, departing next week (recommended)   13,568.00

3. Projected cost of shipping your body to Harvard Medical School via second-day UPS   67.89

4. Adjusted net worth (line 1 minus lines 2 and 3)   _____

5. Projected age at death (see Life Expectancy Table below)   _____

6. Current age   _____

7. Months left to live (line 5 minus line 6, multiplied by 12)   _____

8. Gross monthly nest egg (line 4 divided by line 7) _____

9 Average anticipated monthly income (including Social Security and all other sources, prorated to reflect years remaining) _____

10. Adjusted monthly nest egg (line 8 plus line 9) _____

11. Cost of full-time live-in professional chef, per month (recommended) 8,333.00

12. Cost of leasing matching his-and-hers Mercedes 450SLs, per month (recommended) 1,435.00

13. Monthly living bonus (line 10 minus lines 11 and 12). This is the amount by which you must increase your monthly spending in order to Die Poor. _____

Life Expectancy Table

Current Age	Predicted Age at Death (Male)	Predicted Age at Death (Female)
25	78	84
26	78	84
27	78	84
28	78	84
29	78	84
30	78	84
31	78	84
32	78	84
33	78	84
34	78	84
35	78	84
36	78	84
37	78	84
38	78	84
39	78	85
40	79	85
41	79	85
42	79	85
43	79	85
44	79	85
45	79	85
46	79	85

LIFE EXPECTANCY TABLE

Current Age	Predicted Age at Death (Male)	Predicted Age at Death (Female)
47	79	85
48	79	85
49	79	85
50	79	85
51	79	85
52	79	85
53	80	85
54	80	85
55	80	85
56	80	85
57	80	85
58	80	86
59	81	86
60	81	86
61	81	86
62	81	86
63	81	86
64	82	86
65	82	86
66	82	87
67	82	87
68	83	87
69	83	87
70	83	87

LIFE EXPECTANCY TABLE

Current Age	Predicted Age at Death (Male)	Predicted Age at Death (Female)
71	84	87
72	84	88
73	84	88
74	85	88
75	85	88
76	86	88
77	86	89
78	87	89
79	87	90
80	88	90
81	88	91
82	89	91
83	90	92
84	90	92
85	91	93
86	91	93
87	91	94
88	93	94
89	94	95
90	94	95
91	95	96
92	96	96
93	97	97
94	97	98
95	98	99

You can say
blatantly opinionated things
and no one will argue.

•

It won't be on the exam.

•

You can spend all week
on the crossword puzzle
in the Sunday
New York Times.

•

When you talk,
people call it
oral history.

•

You're ready to do
character work in movies.

•

It's okay to drive
the minimum speed
on the interstate.

•

No more
Christmas shopping—
just write checks.

•

Bad wine tastes like good wine.

•

The Beatles are
putting out records again.

•

Masterpiece Theatre.

•

Lotion-impregnated
toilet paper.

•

Clint Eastwood
has a heart of gold.

•

You have time to watch
all the games on TV.

•

You *can* talk to strangers.

•

You don't have a bedtime.

•

As a kid, you wanted freckles.
Now, you have them—and
they're big.

•

You can carry an umbrella
without fear of retribution.

•

Your secrets are safe
if your friends
can't remember them.

•

Meals with your children
are now a pleasure.

•

In your age bracket,
bell-bottoms are
gone for good.

•

Think of All the Money You're Saving On

Water skis

•

Hotel rooms for afternoon trysts

•

Running shoes

•

Stanley Kaplan

•

Tampons

•

Season tickets

•

Scuba gear

•

Apples, toffee,
and corn on the cob

•

Internet browsers

•

Tuition

•

Sexy underwear

•

Children's clothes

•

Bubble gum

•

Clearasil

•

Birth control pills

•

Cliff Notes

•

Sports cars

•

Roller-coaster rides

•

LSD

•

Sandwich bags

•

Entrance fees for marathons

•

Continuing education

•

Booster shots

•

Lifetime guarantees

•

Baby-sitters

•

Orthodontia

•

Highlights

•

Home pregnancy kits

•

You have no more
plastic accessories,
except for surgical devices.

•

For the first time
since second grade,
your daughter has admitted
that you are right
about something.

•

At least one person
you grew up with
has become sort of famous.

•

Lauren Bacall.

•

Maybe one of your kids
will strike it rich
and buy you a house
in Arizona.

•

Reading the newspaper
can take all morning.

•

Why cook when you can thaw?

•

Why thaw when you can eat out?

•

You're no longer called
upon to reveal your
ignorance of algebra.

•

The guilty pleasure
of throwing away
old wedding presents.

•

Monocles, walking sticks,
and cigarette holders
are no longer affectations.

•

You already own
just the thing to wear
to that funeral.

•

You've had all your shots.

●

You'll never have to make or eat
another school lunch.

●

Heinrich Schliemann,
the excavator of Troy,
became interested
in archaeology at the
age of forty-six.

●

Good-bye
to the PTA.

•

You're less likely to
be arrested for loitering.

•

You'll never wait
in another line at
Disney World.

•

Hospitals and Fabulous Resorts Offer Many of the Same Great Amenities

Expensive rooms

•

Breakfast in bed

•

Foreign-born staff

•

Exercise equipment

•

Scheduled activities

•

Someone to mail
your letters for you

•

Drug use

•

No pets

•

A bathroom close to your bed

•

Gift shop in the lobby

•

Free soap

•

Evening entertainment

•

Revealing attire

•

Help with your luggage

•

Inexplicable surcharges

•

Seemed better
in the brochure

•

You were not
the first person
in your college class
to die.

•

No one blames you
for not recycling.

•

You need less sleep.

•

But you can nap
all you want, anyway.

•

You can't remember
the last time someone gave
you a wedgie.

•

Your baby fat
is gone.

•

No more snowball fights.

•

Your supply of brain cells
is finally down
to a manageable size.

•

Chances grow
smaller every year
that you will die
in childbirth.

•

183

You can go sustaining
in the Junior League.

•

Julie Andrews
still packs a wallop.

•

You can say
"When I was your age . . ."
to more and more people.

•

When you were seventeen,
you didn't think
you'd live this long.

•

The older you get,
the greater your chance
of inheriting money
from your peers.

•

It's now okay to wear
big, soft undies.

•

Single-malt Scotch.

•

Get tan?
Why not!

•

You don't have to worry
about keeping all those
Baldwins straight.

•

You Can Now Enjoy Life's Small Pleasures

Looking for your glasses

•

Noticing the dust on
the picture frames
so you can tell
the maid about it

•

Circling what you want
to watch in *TV Guide*

•

Berating your children,
when they finally call you,
for not having
called you sooner

•

Worrying

•

Entering sweepstakes

•

Thinking about meals

•

Getting ready for meals

•

Meals

•

Complaining about meals

•

Straightening a paper clip
so that you can use it again

•

Wishing you had bought
Berkshire Hathaway
in 1965 at $12 a share

•

Watching the weather report
for every city in which you
have relatives

•

Defrosting

•

Making sure you buy the best kind
of squirrel-proof bird feeder

•

Chatting with the plumber
while he fixes the drips

•

Having long conversations
with your children's
answering machines

•

Gathering lint

•

Looking for a rubber band

•

Bouillon as an entrée

•

Wondering what
cellular phones are for

•

Going to
the post office

•

Giving the day's junk mail
your full consideration

•

Humming along
with the music they play
when they put you on hold

•

You don't have to
pretend to like
spicy food.

•

Your eyes
won't get much worse.

•

Drinking wine every day
turns out to be
good for you.

•

No bikini lines.

•

Your next wife may have a
daughter you can date.

•

"Whatever a man's age,
he can reduce it
several years by putting
a bright-colored flower
in his buttonhole,"
according to Mark Twain.

•

Tagamet, Aleve,
and Rogaine
are now available
without a
prescription.

•

You can go to a party
without worrying
that your skirt
may be sending
the wrong message.

•

Your name isn't
sewn onto the waistband
of your underwear.

•

Paul Cézanne did not
have a major exhibition
until he was sixty-five
(two years before his death).

•

You're older than
authority figures.

•

You can choose
the color of your teeth.

•

You don't have to study history;
you saw it happen.

•

Although you are now older
than all major-league
baseball players, you are still
younger than some
major-league baseball teams.

•

Golf on weekdays.

•

Someone else
will cut your toenails.

•

Your friends are too nearsighted
to notice you're
not wearing makeup.

•

You don't have to finish books.

•

Instead of Counting Sheep When You Can't Sleep at Night, You Can Count

Divorced friends

•

Your IRAs

•

Your grandchildren

•

Friends with
hip replacements

•

Root canals

•

Aching joints

•

Sites that call out
for electrolysis

•

Upcoming
doctors' appointments

•

Pills you forgot to take

•

You're through
with childhood diseases.

•

You don't have to keep up
with popular music.

•

Retin-A.

•

Better yet, Retinova.

•

Even better, glycolic acid peels.

•

If all else fails, face-lifts.

•

And if even *that* doesn't work,
hats with veils.

•

The secret of aging gracefully,
according to Philip Johnson:
"Money helps."

•

Things you buy now
won't wear out.

•

Would you really want
to be twenty again?

•

The number of candles
on your birthday cake
is just an educated guess.

•

If you can't find
that thing you lost,
you can just buy another.

•

No need to have your
color chart done—
you're always winter.

•

Just call the waitress
honey.

•

The joys of nostalgia.

•

Reduced train fares.

•

More and more of your parts
can be replaced.

•

You can't see dandruff.

•

You don't need to
know the words
to the number-one song.

•

Laurence Sterne wrote
Tristram Shandy
when he was in his late forties.

•

You'll never have to go
in-line skating.

•

Yesterday's Youth Icons and Their Birthdates

Hayley Mills
April 18, 1946

Richard Chamberlain
March 31, 1935

Ann-Margret
April 28, 1941

Ron Howard
March 1, 1954

Margaret O'Brien
January 15, 1937

Matt Dillon
February 18, 1964

Mickey Rooney
September 23, 1920

Jerry ("The Beaver") Mathers
June 2, 1948

Desi Arnaz Jr.
January 19, 1953

Robby Benson
January 21, 1955

Yoko Ono
February 18, 1933

Emmanuel *(Webster)* Lewis
March 9, 1971

John Travolta
February 18, 1954

Bjorn Borg
June 6, 1956

Tracy Austin
December 12, 1962

Twiggy
September 19, 1949

Chubby Checker
October 3, 1941

Shirley Temple Black
April 23, 1928

Eloise
October 1955

Sandra Dee
April 23, 1942

Fabian
February 6, 1943

Henry Winkler
October 30, 1945

Brian (Beach Boys) Wilson
June 20, 1942

Bo Derek
November 20, 1956

Dick Clark
November 30, 1939

J. D. Salinger
January 1, 1919

Tatum O'Neal
November 5, 1963

Cher
May 20, 1946

Chastity Bono
March 4, 1969

Joan Baez
January 9, 1941

Stevie Wonder
May 13, 1950

The Cat in the Hat
November 1956

Valerie Bertinelli
April 23, 1960

Mia Farrow
February 9, 1945

Dustin Hoffman
August 1, 1937

Ali MacGraw
April 1, 1938

Eddie Murphy
April 3, 1961

Pat Boone
June 1, 1934

Peter Max
October 19, 1937

Pete Townshend
May 19, 1945

Donny Osmond
December 9, 1957

David McCallum
September 19, 1933

Shelley Fabares
January 19, 1944

John McEnroe
February 16, 1959

John Stamos
August 18, 1963

Tony Danza
April 21, 1951

Miss Peggy Lee
May 26, 1920

Soleil Moon Frye
August 6, 1976

Todd Bridges
May 27, 1965

Tina Yothers
May 5, 1973

Babar
1933

Pippi Longstocking
1950

David Cassidy
April 12, 1950

Peter Fonda
February 23, 1939

Paul McCartney
June 18, 1942

Patty Duke
December 14, 1946

Macaulay Culkin
August 20, 1980

Leif Garrett
November 8, 1961

Brigitte Bardot
September 28, 1934

Carroll Baker
May 28, 1935

Freddie Bartholomew
March 24, 1924

David Letterman
April 12, 1947

Bob Dylan
May 24, 1941

Stevie Nicks
May 26, 1948

Deborah Harry
July 1, 1945

Linda Ronstadt
July 15, 1948

Arlo Guthrie
July 10, 1947

Peggy Fleming
July 27, 1948

Tuesday Weld
August 27, 1948

Frankie Avalon
September 8, 1940

Buy all the candy you want.

•

You don't have to stand
for the national anthem.

•

Instead of plumbing,
angioplasty.

•

Cervantes was in his fifties
when he wrote *Don Quixote*.

•

You can devote
your full attention
to complaining.

•

You can write people
out of your will.

•

Do cobwebs exist
if you can
no longer see them?

•

You can admit
to having liked
On Golden Pond.

•

You can watch for the obituaries
of people you don't like.

•

Every new wrinkle
improves your chances of
beating that speeding ticket.

•

No shelf is too high to
reach with a cane.

•

You don't have to go
to camp anymore.

•

Leave it to Beaver and *I Love Lucy*
are on TV to stay.

•

Barbara Stanwyck movies.

•

Estrogen supplements.

•

Fred Astaire wore a toupee,
and so can you.

•

Many medicines are cheaper
in Mexico.

•

No reason to keep up
with cabinet appointments.

•

You can buy any
toy you want.

•

Deduct your
medical bills.

•

Senior citizens ride
the buses free
at certain times of the day
in Philadelphia.

•

You're Never Too Old to Appear in Your Own Exercise Tape

Just look at:

Linda Evans

•

Jack LaLanne

•

Debbie Reynolds

•

YOU'RE NEVER TOO OLD TO APPEAR IN
YOUR OWN EXERCISE TAPE

Richard Simmons

•

Jane Fonda

•

Christie Brinkley

•

Loni Anderson

•

Dick Van Patten

•

Tom Bosley

•

Cher

•

Raquel Welch

•

Nobody makes
you try new foods.

•

If you can't order it
from a catalog,
you probably
don't need it.

•

Tiffany's sells
lovely pillboxes.

•

You'll never have
to make another costume.

•

Let my belly go.

•

With-it teens think
blue hair is cool.

•

Who needs an alarm clock?

•

Jeanne Calment,
who died in Arles, France,
in 1995 at the age of 121
ate more than two pounds
of chocolate every week.

•

You don't have to
wait up listening for
your children to come in
at night.

•

Great big clip-on earrings.

•

No one expects you to run
into a burning building.

•

It's getting easier and easier
to meet your health-insurance
deductible.

•

Although most parts of
you have shrunk,
your nose, earlobes, and skin
have gotten bigger.

•

Your spouse still snores,
but now you can't hear it.

•

You have plenty of time to write
letters to the editor.

•

You'll never have to buy
another refrigerator.

•

You don't need the shingles
with the thirty-year guarantee.

•

You can just throw
pennies away.

•

Fortunately, You're Now Too Old to Remember

Having your braces tightened

•

Trigonometry

•

Sitting on a phone book
at the dinner table

•

Climbing a spiral staircase
in a miniskirt

•

What you wrote
on your college application—
especially the personal essay

•

Breaking up
at the end of the summer

•

What you looked like at the prom

•

What your first time
was really like

•

Drinking until you threw up

•

Not caring if your hair got wet

•

Worrying about where to sit
in the lunchroom

•

Freshman mixers

•

Shag haircuts

•

The name of the one
your mother wanted you to marry

•

Hating how skinny you were

•

Waiting and waiting
for the phone to ring

•

Waiting and waiting
for your period

•

Expressing breast milk

•

The name of that whatever

•

Sitting at the children's table
on Thanksgiving

•

Being turned down
for a car loan

•

Your first marriage

•

The statute of limitations
has probably expired.

•

Do they make quadrifocals?

•

If you wait long enough,
even bad stocks go up.

•

You're less and less likely
to be the victim of bullies.

•

The bus driver expects you
to ask nervous questions
about your stop.

•

Why *not* wear panty hose
with pants?

•

A pint of ice cream
lasts all month.

•

You can wear your glasses
in the pool.

•

You really *have* watched
a lovelier sunset,
eaten a sweeter peach, and
seen a more beautiful baby.

•

You can remember
the flood of '55.

•

People have stopped
taping KICK ME signs
to your rear end.

•

Someone has to buy padded
hangers and drawer sachets.

•

You know enough
about the Bloomsbury set
to last you the rest of your life.

•

Abraham Lincoln was a
Republican.

•

No need to pay a psychic
to see your future—
you've already lived it.

•

If your pants fall down
while you're dancing,
you'll be a cinch to get on
America's Funniest Home Videos.

•

You Might as Well Just Throw Away

Leftover rolls of wallpaper

•

Photographs of
people whose names
you don't remember

•

Old ballgowns

•

Jigsaw puzzles

•

Maternity clothes

•

Tube tops

•

Extra curry powder

•

Anything that needs
to be repaired

•

Canceled checks
from decades
that time forgot

•

That shaving brush you got for
Christmas twenty years ago

•

Your children's old schoolwork

•

All remaining beach toys
and hamster cages

•

Diplomas

•

Your pasta machine

•

Anything covered
with frost in the freezer

•

Fountain pens

•

Gladiator sandals

•

Typewriters

•

Nehru jackets

•

Maxi-coats

•

Hot pants

•

The fancy guest soap

•

Old belts

•

School uniforms

•

Wire hangers

•

Clogs

•

Frye boots

•

Badminton equipment

•

Leather pants

•

Old issues of *National Geographic*
and *Gourmet*

•

You can get rid
of that car seat.

•

The Little League will continue
to get along just fine
without your help.

•

You don't have to do the polka,
the shimmy, the hokey pokey,
the twist, the jerk, the Watusi,
or the macarena.

•

Vitamin B$_{12}$ shots can't hurt
and might help.

•

No more baby-sitters
to drive home.

•

You can have the
cable company block
Barney from your TV.

•

Maybe you'll have
a nice roommate.

•

Cough drops
come in many
interesting flavors.

•

Nobody reads the
fine print,
anyway.

•

Someone else
will have to bury your pets.

•

You have a whole new
appreciation for
Betty White.

•

People are impressed
if you know *anything*
about professional sports.

•

Anyone ten years older

or younger

is now the same

age as you.

•

No more parades.

•

You have a profound new

respect for your knees.

•

Making it through
airport security
is easier than ever.

•

You can remember when
dangerous sex wasn't dangerous.

•

With fewer friends,
you have fewer birthdays
and anniversaries
to remember.

•

Great Things to Talk About

Digestive challenges

•

Whether the weather is better or
worse than it used to be

•

Medigap insurance

•

The cost of burial plots

•

The size of prostate glands

•

Codicils

•

Ingratitude

•

Chairs in the lobby

•

Various conspiracies

•

The ingredients of urine

•

Why Johnny can't read,
write, add, subtract, converse,
appreciate the past,
or say thank-you

•

The tax consequences
of living for ten more years

•

Side effects

•

Whether that baby
is dressed warmly enough

•

The main problem
with everything nowadays

•

Irrevocable powers of attorney

•

No more pregnancy scares.

•

Standing in the shallow end
counts as swimming.

•

There's nothing left to learn
the hard way.

•

You're finished for good
with homework.

•

Preparation H is now
a multi-use product.

•

Dry toast and
cottage cheese
make a meal.

•

No more
piggyback rides.

•

You might as well lie
about your children's ages, too.

•

You can't regret
what you don't remember.

•

You are of
steadily increasing
interest to medical research.

•

Everyone looks out
for orphans—
and now you are one.

•

Might as well snooze
until dessert.

•

Many of your current ailments
were incurable
when you were young.

•

The size of the
MacArthur Foundation's
"genius awards" increases
with the age of
the recipients.

•

If you say you coined
the word *software*,
your grandchildren
may believe you.

•

Your high school reunions
are less crowded than
they used to be.

•

Most of life's
major disappointments
are now behind you.

•

Your children are starting
to like you again.

•

Times When You May Want to Lie About Your Age

While prospecting for
a second, third, or fourth spouse

•

When auditioning
for work as an actor or actress

•

On the eve of your next birthday

•

When filling out authors'
questionnaires

•

When you'd rather pay full price for
a ticket than admit you're sixty-five

•

When taking a driving test

•

When the young dental assistant
asking your vital statistics is cute

•

When your children
begin to lie about their ages

•

In flattering light

•

Whenever you can get
away with it

•

Good old Willard Scott.

•

You can be the first to arrive
and the first to leave.

•

Your joints are
more accurate than the
National Weather Service.

•

At your age,
a small tattoo can have
a big impact.

•

Because you can
remember when a dollar
really was a dollar,
looking at your
bank statement makes
you feel rich.

•

You don't have to stand
when someone stops
by your table to say hello.

•

Been there, done that—
and you have
the slides to prove it.

•

At parties, no one tries
to pick up your spouse.

•

According to a study
from the University of
Southern California,
regular exercise
can turn your clock
back twenty-five years.

•

You already know
how it's going
to turn out.

•

A microwave oven
is more useful than a
personal computer.

•

Nobody calls you Sport
anymore.

•

You'll never have to assemble
another bicycle on
Christmas Eve.

•

Voting is simpler
now that Medicare
and Social Security
are the only issues that matter.

•

Someday, Aquasize and
Slimnastics will be
Olympic events.

•

Peter Jennings seems like
such a nice man.

•

Great Birthdays

Twenty-one at Last

Your permanent record
no longer matters.

•

Order a sidecar or a
grasshopper—it's legal

•

You can probably still
get student discounts.

•

Next year you can wear
sweatshirts from other colleges.

•

You can screw up for a few more
years and still turn out okay.

•

You can be a grown-up or a kid,
depending on your mood.

•

Going to job interviews
is more fun than going to work.

•

Juvenile detention center?
Never again!

•

A great excuse for a party.

•

Hooray! You're Thirty!

You still feel like a teenager.

•

You are not yet as fat
as you are going to be.

•

You are fully vested
in your company's
retirement plan.

•

Expense-account dining.

•

In public opinion surveys,
you can still check
the 21–30 box.

•

A hundred thousand dollars
still seems like a lot of money.

•

A great excuse for a party.

•

Finally Forty

People assumed you were lying
when you were thirty-nine, anyway.

•

Forty and *fabulous*
just go together.

•

The spa decade.

•

There's more to eat at parties
than pretzels.

•

No more pressure to be
the wunderkind.

•

Still young enough
to procreate.

•

The friends you lust for
will soon be divorced.

•

You have more
frequent flier miles
than you can use up
by yourself.

•

You can stay in bed later
than your kids.

•

You own all the essential
household appliances.

•

A great excuse
for a party.

•

How did you ever
live without
the self-care catalog?

•

You already know better
than to order X-Ray Spex
or Sea Monkeys.

•

Think of all the people
who haven't seen
your snapshots yet.

•

Meals on Wheels.

•

Supp-Hose.

•

Mark Twain said wrinkles are
where smiles used to be.

•

You can hold
your grandchildren
spellbound with tales
about black-and-white TV.

•

When your wife says
she's late, she means
she's constipated.

•

Disappointment
is less disappointing.

•

You're less and less likely
to be subjected to a strip search.

•

People have stopped
trying to teach you
new tricks.

•

After years of
asking your children
to turn the TV down,
you are now asking them
to turn it up.

•

Arizona doesn't seem
too hot in the
summer anymore.

•

No one has the authority
to send you
to your room.

•

Your friends look more and
more like you.

•

No one except
your husband and
certain medical personnel
will ever see
your belly button.

•

You can wear
a sombrero
and a bathrobe
at the beach.

•

Hair Tips
for Those
Over Forty

If it looked good on Annette
Funicello, it's got to work on you.

•

If it looks good on
Annette Bening,
it may not look good on you.

•

Never use a home hair color
called Burnt Offering.

•

Split ends make
hair look thicker.

•

Long bangs are
an inexpensive alternative
to an eye lift.

•

If it looks like a toupee,
it might as well be a toupee
(compare David Letterman
and Marv Albert).

•

Why be the president of
the Hair Club for Men
when you can just be
a member?

•

Mousse for men
is a no-no.

•

No long hair over fifty,
except for the following:

Jane Fonda
Renata Adler
Gloria Steinem
Diana Ross
Georgia O'Keeffe
Goldie Hawn
Suzanne Somers
Edith Wharton
Cher
Benjamin Franklin

As the years go by,
you'll have chances
to become
better acquainted
with your children's
attorneys.

•

Your house doesn't
get messy anymore.

•

Old people live longer
than young people.
(A newborn girl's life
expectancy is seventy-two;
an eighty-year-old
woman's is ninety.)

•

No one will ever call you
callow again.

•

Letting the waist out
makes clothes seem new.

•

No more post-Christmas
letdown.

•

When you watch the sun rise
now, you're not lying next to
a stranger on the beach
with sand in your underpants.

•

The convenience of having your
own oxygen supply.

•

People don't do double takes
when you put on your
flowered bathing cap.

•

Protesters are less likely
to throw paint
on your fur coat.

•

You can go to the grocery store
in a raincoat and a slip.

•

At last you're old enough
to treat servants like servants.

•

Gardening.

•

Reread your favorite books
as though for the first time.

•

No more fast dancing.

•

Why *not* buy furniture
that reclines?

•

Older women
dating younger men
are assumed
to be great in bed.

•

Great Messages to Carve on Your Gravestone

Here lies an Atheist
All dressed up
And no place to go
(Thurmont, Maryland)

Here lies
Johnny Yeast
Pardon Me
For Not Rising
(Ruidoso, New Mexico)

Haine
Haint

(Epitaph of Arthur Haine,
Vancouver, Washington)

Here lies the body
of Jonathan Blake
Stepped on the gas
Instead of the brake

(Uniondale, Pennsylvania)

The defense rests

(Epitaph of an attorney,
Rockford, Illinois)

Gone, but not forgiven
(Epitaph of an adulterous man,
written by his widow,
Atlanta, Georgia)

No hits, no runs, no heirs
(Epitaph of an old maid,
Scranton, Pennsylvania)

"I told you I didn't
feel so good"
(Epitaph of the ultimate
guilt-tripping mother)

That is all
(London)

Older men dating younger
women are assumed to be rich.

•

Bridge keeps your mind sharp
and may ward off senility.

•

You have more and more
chances to meet
attractive doctors.

•

You can finally buy shoes
that don't hurt your feet.

•

It's getting easier
to hit your
aerobic target heart rate.

•

You can wear a bathing suit
with a skirt.

•

Pity is almost as flattering
as admiration.

•

Old people are
never picked for
audience participation.

•

There's time now
to read *War and Peace*.

•

In the South, they call you
Ma'am or Sir.

•

No one tells you
to grow up.

•

Skip those
Broadway revivals—
you saw the originals
at a tenth the price.

•

You can stop upgrading
your software.

•

You can explain
what communism was.

•

Wild animals can smell fear,
but they can't smell
forgetfulness.

•

You own antiques after all.

•

You are less likely to be stalked.

•

Charles Darwin was
in his fifties when he published
The Origin of Species.

•

It's too late to sell out.

•

The World Isn't Getting Older; It's Getting Better

Federal Express

•

Televised trials

•

The Wonder Bra

•

Laser hair removal

•

Michael Milken, convicted felon

•

Starbucks

•

Caller ID

•

The discovery that walking
is as good for you as running

•

New crayon colors

•

Quicken

•

Four-wheel drive

•

Tangerine jellybeans

•

ESPN-2

•

Post-Its

•

Microwave ovens

•

More stylish maternity clothes

•

Parabolic skis

•

Häagen-Dazs sorbets

•

Videotaped everything

•

Life on Mars

•

Polar fleece

•

Movie reservations by phone

•

E-mail

•

Much shorter wars

•

Royal divorce

•

Barnes & Noble, Borders,
and Amazon.com

•

Prozac

•

Self-adhesive postage stamps

•

Suitcases with wheels

•

Go ahead and order
the rice pudding.
You've earned the right.

•

Not another word from
Nietzsche or Kierkegaard.

•

Good-bye to science fairs.

•

Jury duty seems like a treat.

•

If you were a
Supreme Court justice,
you'd still be working.

•

Your friends praise you
for the accomplishments
of your children.

•

Why doesn't everyone
have a chair in the shower?

•

When you marry again,
they won't print your age
in the *New York Times*.

•

No one expects you
to remember your haftarah.

•

Advertisers have stopped
targeting you.

•

You can sit up in bed
just by pushing a button.

•

You always get
the comfiest chair
in the room.

•

If you still have your soul,
you'll probably keep it.

•

You don't have to pretend
to like depressing movies.

•

Birthdays are more fun
now that you buy
your own presents.

•

You won't be asked
to host the block party.

•

Liver spots are just
human patina.

•

When you were a kid,
you dreamed of having your
own nitroglycerin.

•

You've seen it all before,
even if you don't
remember where.

•

Everything I Need to Know I Learned at the North Pole: Ten Lessons from Santa Claus, the Oldest Living Human

You don't have to spend
the winter in Florida.

•

Dress in cheerful colors.

•

Lose the girdle.

•

Stay married.

•

Go out of your way
to be kind to children.

•

Keep working,
even if only part time.

•

Let others
do the heavy lifting.

•

See the world.

•

Smoke a pipe
if you feel like it.

•

Don't forget
the ho-ho-ho.

•

It's nice to have a railing
to hold on to
in the bathtub.

•

Think of gray hair
as a blank slate.

•

Time to consider
an artificial Christmas tree.

•

Your most creative tax returns
can no longer be audited.

•

You'll never have to buy
more twine, wood glue,
calamine lotion, pliers,
Tabasco sauce, or nutmeg.

•

At your last checkup,
your doctor suggested
that you *gain* some weight.

•

Your peer group
exerts less pressure.

•

Senior tennis.

•

Daniel Defoe did not
begin to write books
until he was
almost sixty.

•

You look great in a tuxedo.

•

You aren't necessarily
as old as you feel.

•

Wisdom.

•

A funeral is a good place
to catch up with old friends.

•

Who says you can't wear
black socks with shorts
and sneakers?

•

The alternative is worse.

•